B♭ Bass Clarinet

# Muscle Memory Exercises for Band

by Randy & Ami Kulik

P.O. Box 517    Glenmoore, PA 19343
Voice: 610-942-2370    Fax: 610-942-0660
Email: info@nemusicpub.com  ♪  Web: www.nemusicpub.com
1 2 3 4 5 6 7 8 17 16 15 14 13 12 11 10
Printed in the United States of America

Copyright © 2010 by Northeastern Music Publications, Inc.
All rights reserved. This book may not be reproduced by any means, whole or in part, without written permission from the publisher.

Layout & Design by RoLin Graphics

# Introduction

Muscle Memory is a concept that allows you to be an active participant in your musical education. If you were like us when we were kids, we would totally zone out every time our directors asked us to look at the key signature after we played a wrong note on our instruments! It's okay. It's not your fault! We wanted our directors to tell us what we were doing wrong. The *Muscle Memory Method* will teach you what to do.

- Muscle Memory allows you to create your scales and key signatures with the scale worksheets and develop the physical skills to play your scales accurately. The worksheets will also help you understand key signatures. You will be able to read music better.

  Look for the "brain" for memory tips in each lesson.

  Sharps= **F**at **C**ats **G**o **D**own **A**lleys **E**ating **B**irds

  Flats= **BEAD G**reat **C**hicago **F**ire

- Through the *Muscle Memory* physical activities, you will be shown a way to correct your mistakes and make it easier to play your band music.

   Look for the "exercise bars" for the Muscle Memory Exercise-MME.

- The *Practice to Performance* exercises are designed to help you learn to play your scales from memory.

  Look for the "horn" for the Practice to Performance exercise-PTP.

- The *Practice to Performance* chorales will give you a chance to practice your PTP exercises with your full band or a small group.

  Your band director will decide how to play these.

  **PTP Chorale**
  **Traditional Chorale**
  **Melody in Bass Chorale**

- At the end of the book, you will find all the major scales to help you practice.

B♭ Bass Clarinet

After a little practice with this book you'll be able to play your scales more easily and in less time.  You'll play the right notes more often because YOU will know how to correct your mistakes.  Band will be more fun for you because you will know what you're doing.  You'll be able to think about making music instead of worrying about playing wrong notes and your band director will be happy because you will be playing the right notes and reading music.  Have fun!

Ami and Randy Kulik

## Where to find it...

Page
- 2. Introduction
- 4. Key Signatures
- 5. F (Concert E♭) Major Scale
- 6. B♭ (Concert A♭) Major Scale
- 7. E♭ (Concert D♭) Major Scale
- 8. A♭ (Concert G♭) Major Scale
- 9. D♭ (Concert C♭) Major Scale
- 10. C (Concert B♭) Major Scale
- 11. G (Concert F) Major Scale
- 12. D (Concert C) Major Scale
- 13. A (Concert G) Major Scale
- 14. E (Concert D) Major Scale
- 15. B (Concert A) Major Scale
- 16. F♯ (Concert E) Major Scale
- 17. F (Concert E♭) Chromatic
- 18. C♯ (Concert B) Major Scale (Enharmonic D♭)
- 19. G♭ (Concert E) Major Scale Enharmonic F♯)
- 20. C♭ (Concert A) Major Scale (Enharmonic B)
- 21. PTP Exercises for All Keys
- 23. All Major Scales and the Chromatic Scale

B♭ Bass Clarinet

# Key Signature Rules

Order of Flats: B♭, E♭, A♭, D♭, G♭, C♭ F♭

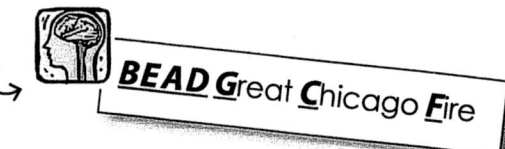
**BEAD G**reat **C**hicago **F**ire

### KEY SIGNATURE – FLAT RULE:

Go through the order of flats until you get to the name of your key and add one more. That will give you all the flats in the key signature.

EXAMPLE:  Key of A♭

Say the flats: B♭ – E♭ –(A♭)– add one more – D♭
The key of A♭ has four flats: B♭, E♭, A♭, D♭

| Key of: | Flats |
|---|---|
| F (1♭) | B♭ |
| B♭ (2♭) | B♭, E♭ |
| E♭ (3♭) | B♭ E♭ A♭ |
| A♭ (4♭) | B♭ E♭ A♭ D♭ |
| D♭ (5♭) | B♭ E♭ A♭ D♭ G♭ |
| G♭ (6♭) | B♭ E♭ A♭ D♭ G♭ C♭ |
| C♭ (7♭) | B♭ E♭ A♭ D♭ G♭ C♭ F♭ |

Order of Sharps: F#, C#, G#, D#, A#, E#, B#

**F**at **C**ats **G**o **D**own **A**lleys **E**ating **B**irds

### KEY SIGNATURE – SHARP RULE:

Name the sharp that's ½ step lower than the name of your key, and that's the last sharp in the key signature.

EXAMPLE:  Key of D
The sharp that is ½ step lower = C#
The key of D has two sharps: F#, C#

| Key of: | Sharps |
|---|---|
| G (1#) | F# |
| D (2#) | F# C# |
| A (3#) | F# C# G# |
| E (4#) | F# C# G# D# |
| B (5#) | F# C# G# D# A# |
| F# (6#) | F# C# G# D# A# E# |
| C# (7#) | F# C# G# D# A# E# B# |

Memory Tip

Key of E♭: **Repeat to yourself or out loud:**
"E♭ has 3 flats, E♭ has 3 flats – B♭, E♭, A♭"

Look for these Memory Tips in each lesson.

Name of **your** scale _____

The 1st note of the scale is the "name of **your** scale"

Name the notes of the Scale:
___  ___  ___  ___  ___  ___  ___  ___

The B♭ Bass Clarinet is a B♭ instrument. The "concert pitch" is one whole step lower than the name of your scale. When you play **your** "C", the **actual** pitch is concert B♭

# F (Concert E♭) Major Scale

**BEAD G**reat **C**hicago **F**ire
Go through the order of flats until you get to the name of your key and add one more. That will give you all the flats in the key signature.

**Scale Work Sheet**

Concert Pitch ____

Name of your scale

_____

Name the notes of the Scale:

___  ___  ___  ___  ___  ___  ___  ___

Key Signature: Name the flat

____

1. Write the key signature, measure bars and choose a time signature.
2. Write the scale using music notation. Use different note values to create a scale song.

 **Muscle Memory Exercise (MME): F (Concert E♭)**
1. <u>Without playing</u> your instrument, Practice fingering **A** to **B♭**.
2. <u>Without playing</u> your instrument Practice fingering **B♭** to **C**.
3. Practice fingering the MME [**A-B♭-C-B♭-A**] 4 times on your instrument.

 **Memory Tip**
Key of F: **Repeat to yourself or out loud:**
F has 1 flat, F has 1 flat–B♭

 **Practice to Performance (PTP)**
1. Play the PTP exercise 4 times.
2. Turn to page 21 and play the PTP exercise #1.

5

B♭ Bass Clarinet

# B♭ (Concert A♭) Major Scale

**BEAD Great Chicago Fire**
Go through the order of flats until you get to the name of your key and add one more. That will give you all the flats in the key signature.

**Scale Work Sheet**

Concert Pitch ____

Name of your scale
_____

Name the notes of the Scale:
__ __ __ __ __ __ __ __

Key Signature :
Name the flats

__ __

1. Write the key signature, measure bars and choose a time signature.
2. Write the scale using music notation. Use different note values to create a scale song.

**Muscle Memory Exercise (MME):** *B♭ (Concert A♭)*
1. <u>Without playing</u> your instrument, Practice fingering *D* to *E♭*.
2. <u>Without playing</u> your instrument Practice fingering *E♭* to *F*.
3. Practice fingering the MME [*D-E♭-F-E♭-D*] 4 times on your instrument.

**Memory Tip**
Key of B♭: **Repeat to yourself or out loud:**
B♭ has 2 flats, B♭ has 2 flats – B♭ E♭

**Practice to Performance (PTP)**
1. Play the PTP exercise 4 times.
2. Turn to page 21 and play PTP exercise #2.

6

B♭ Bass Clarinet

# E♭ (Concert D♭) Major Scale

 **BEAD Great Chicago Fire**
Go through the order of flats until you get to the name of your key and add one more. That will give you all the flats in the key signature.

**Scale Work Sheet**

Concert Pitch ____

Name of your scale
_____

Name the notes of the Scale:
__  __  __  __  __  __  __  __

Key Signature : Name the flats
____  ____  ____

1. Write the key signature, measure bars and choose a time signature.
2. Write the scale using music notation. Use different note values to create a scale song.

**Muscle Memory Exercise (MME):** E♭ (Concert D♭)

1. <u>Without playing</u> your instrument, Practice fingering **G** to **A♭**.
2. <u>Without playing</u> your instrument Practice fingering **A♭** to **B♭**.
3. Practice fingering the MME [**G-A♭-B♭-A♭-G**] 4 times on your instrument.

 **Memory Tip**
Key of E♭: **Repeat to yourself or out loud:**
E♭ has 3 flats, E♭ has 3 flats – B♭ E♭ A♭

**Practice to Performance (PTP)**

1. Play the PTP exercise 4 times.
2. Turn to page 21 and play PTP exercise #3.

7

B♭ Bass Clarinet

# A♭ (Concert G♭) Major Scale

**BEAD G**reat **C**hicago **F**ire
Go through the order of flats until you get to the name of your key and add one more. That will give you all the flats in the key signature.

## Scale Work Sheet

Concert Pitch ____

Name of your scale
_____

Key Signature: Name the flats

____  ____  ____  ____

1. Write the key signature, measure bars and choose a time signature.
2. Write the scale using music notation. Use different note values to create a scale song.

Name the notes of the Scale:

____  ____  ____  ____  ____  ____  ____  ____

---

### Muscle Memory Exercise (MME): A♭ (Concert G♭)

1. <u>Without playing</u> your instrument, Practice fingering **C** to **D♭**.
2. <u>Without playing</u> your instrument Practice fingering **D♭** to **E♭**.
3. Practice fingering the MME [**C-D♭-E♭-D♭-C**] 4 times on your instrument.

### Practice to Performance (PTP)

1. Play the PTP exercise 4 times.
2. Turn to page 21 and play PTP exercise #4.

 **Memory Tip**

Key of A♭: **Repeat to yourself or out loud:**
A♭ has 4 flats, A♭ has 4 flats – B♭ E♭ A♭ D♭

8

B♭ Bass Clarinet

# D♭ (Concert C♭) Major Scale

**BEAD **G**reat **C**hicago **F**ire
Go through the order of flats until you get to the name of your key and add one more. That will give you all the flats in the key signature.

**Scale Work Sheet**

Concert Pitch _____

Name of your scale

_____

Name the notes of the Scale:

___  ___  ___  ___  ___  ___  ___  ___

Key Signature :
Name the flats

___  ___  ___  ___  ___

1. Write the key signature, measure bars and choose a time signature.
2. Write the scale using music notation. Use different note values to create a scale song.

### Muscle Memory Exercise (MME): D♭ (Concert C♭)
1. <u>Without playing</u> your instrument, Practice fingering **F** to **G♭**.
2. <u>Without playing</u> your instrument Practice fingering **G♭** to **A♭**.
3. Practice fingering the MME [**F**-**G♭**-**A♭**-**G♭**-**F**] 4 times on your instrument.

### Practice to Performance (PTP)
1. Play the PTP exercise 4 times.
2. Turn to page 21 and play PTP exercise #5.

**Memory Tip**

Key of D♭: *Repeat to yourself or out loud:*
D♭ has 5 flats, D♭ has 5 flats – B♭ E♭ A♭ D♭ G♭

**PTP Chorale**

**Traditional Chorale**

**Melody in Bass Chorale**

9

B♭ Bass Clarinet

# C (Concert B♭) Major Scale

## Scale Work Sheet

Concert Pitch _____

Name of your scale

_____

Name the notes of the Scale:

___  ___  ___  ___  ___  ___  ___  ___

1. Write the key signature, measure bars and choose a time signature.
2. Write the scale using music notation. Use different note values to create a scale song.

 **Muscle Memory Exercise (MME): C (Concert B♭)**
1. <u>Without playing</u> your instrument, Practice fingering *A* to *B natural (♮)*.
2. <u>Without playing</u> your instrument Practice fingering *B♮* to *C*.
3. Practice fingering the MME [*A-B♮-C-B♮-A*] 4 times on your instrument.

 **Practice to Performance (PTP)**
1. Play the PTP exercise 4 times.
2. Turn to page 22 and play PTP exercise #1.

**Memory Tip**

Key of C: *Repeat to yourself or out loud:*
I "C" (see) no sharps,
I "C" (see) no flats.

10

B♭ Bass Clarinet

# G (Concert F) Major Scale

**F**at **C**ats **G**o **D**own
**A**lleys **E**ating **B**irds

Name the sharp that's ½ step lower than the name of your key, and that's the last sharp in the key signature.

Concert Pitch _____

Name of your scale
_____

Name the notes of the Scale:

___  ___  ___  ___  ___  ___  ___  ___

Key Signature: Name the Sharp

_____

1. Write the key signature, measure bars and choose a time signature.
2. Write the scale using music notation. Use different note values to create a scale song.

**Scale Work Sheet**

 **Muscle Memory Exercise (MME): G (Concert F)**
1. Without playing your instrument, Practice fingering *E* to *F♯*.
2. Without playing your instrument Practice fingering *F♯* to *G*.
3. Practice fingering the MME [*E-F♯-G-F♯-E*] 4 times on your instrument.

 **Practice to Performance (PTP)**
1. Play the PTP exercise 4 times.
2. Turn to page 22 and play PTP exercise #2.

 **Memory Tip**

Key of G: **Repeat to yourself or out loud:**
G has 1 sharp, G has 1 sharp – F♯

**PTP Chorale**

**Traditional Chorale**

**Melody in Bass Chorale**

11

B♭ Bass Clarinet

# D (Concert C) Major Scale

**Fat Cats Go Down Alleys Eating Birds**
Name the sharp that's ½ step lower than the name of your key, and that's the last sharp in the key signature.

Concert Pitch _____

Name of your scale
_____

Name the notes of the Scale:
_ _ _ _ _ _ _ _

Key Signature : Name the sharps
___ ___

1. Write the key signature, measure bars and choose a time signature.
2. Write the scale using music notation. Use different note values to create a scale song.

Scale Work Sheet

## Muscle Memory Exercise (MME): D (Concert C)

1. <u>Without playing</u> your instrument, Practice fingering **B** to **C♯**.
2. <u>Without playing</u> your instrument Practice fingering **C♯** to **D**.
3. Practice fingering the MME [**B-C♯-D-C♯-B**] 4 times on your instrument.

## Practice to Performance (PTP)

1. Play the PTP exercise 4 times.
2. Turn to page 22 and play PTP exercise #3.

### Memory Tip
Key of D: **Repeat to yourself or out loud:**
D has 2 sharps, D has 2 sharps – F♯ C♯

**PTP Chorale**

**Traditional Chorale**

**Melody in Bass Chorale**

12

B♭ Bass Clarinet

# A (Concert G) Major Scale

**F**at **C**ats **G**o **D**own
**A**lleys **E**ating **B**irds

Name the sharp that's ½ step lower than the name of your key, and that's the last sharp in the key signature.

## Scale Work Sheet

Concert Pitch _____

Name of your scale

_____

Name the notes of the Scale:

___ ___ ___ ___ ___ ___ ___ ___

Key Signature:
Name the sharps

___ ___ ___

1. Write the key signature, measure bars and choose a time signature.
2. Write the scale using music notation. Use different note values to create a scale song.

## Muscle Memory Exercise (MME): A (Concert G)

1. <u>Without playing</u> your instrument, Practice fingering *F♯* to *G♯*.
2. <u>Without playing</u> your instrument Practice fingering *G♯* to *A*.
3. Practice fingering the MME [*F♯-G♯-A-G♯-F♯*] 4 times on your instrument.

### Memory Tip

Key of A: ***Repeat to yourself or out loud:***
A has 3 sharps, A has 3 sharps – F♯ C♯ G♯

## Practice to Performance (PTP)

1. Play the PTP exercise 4 times.
2. Turn to page 22 and play PTP exercise #4.

13

Bb Bass Clarinet

# E (Concert D) Major Scale

**Scale Work Sheet**

**Fat Cats Go Down Alleys Eating Birds**
Name the sharp that's ½ step lower than the name of your key, and that's the last sharp in the key signature.

Concert Pitch _____

Name of your scale
_____

Name the notes of the Scale:
___ ___ ___ ___ ___ ___ ___ ___

Key Signature: Name the sharps
___ ___ ___ ___

1. Write the key signature, measure bars and choose a time signature.
2. Write the scale using music notation. Use different note values to create a scale song.

### Muscle Memory Exercise (MME): E (Concert D)
1. <u>Without playing</u> your instrument, Practice fingering *C#* to *D#*.
2. <u>Without playing</u> your instrument Practice fingering *D#* to *E*.
3. Practice fingering the MME [*C#-D#-E-D#-C#*] 4 times on your instrument.

### Practice to Performance (PTP)
1. Play the PTP exercise 4 times.
2. Turn to page 22 and play PTP exercise #5.

**Memory Tip**
Key of E: **Repeat to yourself or out loud:**
E has 4 sharps, E has 4 sharps – F# C# G# D#

14

B♭ Bass Clarinet

# B (Concert A) Major Scale

**Fat Cats Go Down Alleys Eating Birds**
Name the sharp that's ½ step lower than the name of your key, and that's the last sharp in the key signature.

**Scale Work Sheet**

Concert Pitch _____

Name of your scale
_____

Name the notes of the Scale:
___ ___ ___ ___ ___ ___ ___ ___

Key Signature :
Name the sharps
___ ___ ___ ___ ___

1. Write the key signature, measure bars and choose a time signature.
2. Write the scale using music notation. Use different note values to create a scale song.

### Muscle Memory Exercise (MME): B (Concert A)
1. <u>Without playing</u> your instrument, Practice fingering *G♯* to *A♯*.
2. <u>Without playing</u> your instrument Practice fingering *A♯* to *B*.
3. Practice fingering the MME [*G♯-A♯-B-A♯-G♯*] 4 times on your instrument.

**Memory Tip**
Key of B: **Repeat to yourself or out loud:**
B has 5 sharps, B has 5 sharps– F♯ C♯ G♯ D♯ A♯

### Practice to Performance (PTP)
1. Play the PTP exercise 4 times.
2. Turn to page 22 and play PTP exercise #6

**PTP Chorale**

**Traditional Chorale**

**Melody in Bass Chorale**

15

Bb Bass Clarinet

# F#(Concert E) Major Scale

**F**at **C**ats **G**o **D**own **A**lleys **E**ating **B**irds
Name the sharp that's ½ step lower than the name of your key, and that's the last sharp in the key signature.

**Scale Work Sheet**

Concert Pitch ____

Name of your scale
_____

Name the notes of the Scale:
__ __ __ __ __ __ __ __

 Key Signature: Name the sharps
_____

1. Write the key signature, measure bars and choose a time signature.
2. Write the scale using music notation. Use different note values to create a scale song.

## Muscle Memory Exercise (MME): F# (Concert E)

1. <u>Without playing</u> your instrument, practice fingering *D#* to *E#*.
2. <u>Without playing</u> your instrument practice fingering *E#* to *F#*.
3. Practice fingering the MME [*D#-E#-F#-E#-D#*] 4 times on your instrument.

 **Memory Tip**

Key of F#: **Repeat to yourself or out loud:**
F# has 6 sharps, F# has 6 sharps – F# C# G# D# A# E#

## Practice to Performance (PTP)

1. Play the PTP exercise 4 times.
2. Turn to page 22 and play PTP exercise #7

16

# F (Concert E♭) Chromatic Scale

 **BEAD Great Chicago Fire**
Go through the order of flats until you get to the name of your key and add one more. That will give you all the flats in the key signature.

**Scale Work Sheet**

Concert Pitch ____

Name of your scale

_____  ____

Key Signature :
Name the flat

Name the notes of the ascending (going up) chromatic scale, followed by the descending chromatic scale (going down). Use your enharmonic relationship chart if you need help.

___ ___ ___ ___ ___ ___ ___ ___ ___ ___

___ ___ ___ ___ ___ ___ ___ ___ ___ ___

1. Write the key signature, measure bars and choose a time signature.
2. Write the scale using music notation. Use different note values to create a scale song.

 Memory Tip

**Enharmonic Relationships**
C♯=D♭ | D♯=E♭ | E=F♭ | E♯=F | F♯=G♭ | G♯=A♭ | A♯=B♭ | B=C♭ | B♯=C

 **Practice to Performance (PTP)**
1. Play the PTP exercise 4 times.

17

Bb Bass Clarinet

# C#(Concert B) Major Scale
## (Enharmonic D♭)

**Fat Cats Go Down Alleys Eating Birds**
Name the sharp that's ½ step lower than the name of your key, and that's the last sharp in the key signature.

Concert Pitch _____

Name of your scale
_____

Name the notes of the Scale:
_____

Key Signature: Name the sharps
_____ _____ _____ _____ _____ _____ _____

1. Write the key signature, measure bars and choose a time signature.
2. Write the scale using music notation. Use different note values to create a scale song.

Scale Work Sheet

## Memory Tip

Key of C#: **Repeat to yourself or out loud:**
C# has 7 sharps, C# has 7 sharps – F# C# G# D# A# E# B#.
I "C" (see) all sharps.

### Muscle Memory Exercise (MME): C#(Concert B)
1. <u>Without playing</u> your instrument, Practice fingering A# to B#.
2. <u>Without playing</u> your instrument Practice fingering B# to C#.
3. Practice fingering the MME [A#-B#-C#-B#-A#] 4 times on your instrument.

### Practice to Performance (PTP)
1. Play the PTP exercise 4 times.
2. Turn to page 22 and play PTP exercise #8.

18

B♭ Bass Clarinet

# G♭ (Concert E) Major Scale
## (Enharmonic F♯)

 **_BEAD G_**reat **_C_**hicago **_F_**ire
Go through the order of flats until you get to the name of your key and add one more. That will give you all the flats in the key signature.

Scale Work Sheet

Concert Pitch _____

Name of your scale
_____

Name the notes of the Scale:
___  ___  ___  ___  ___  ___  ___  ___

Key Signature : Name the flats
___ ___ ___ ___ ___ ___

1. Write the key signature, measure bars and choose a time signature.
2. Write the scale using music notation. Use different note values to create a scale song.

 **Memory Tip**

Key of G♭: *Repeat to yourself or out loud:*
G♭ has 6 flats, G♭ has 6 flats – B♭ E♭ A♭ D♭ G♭ C♭

 **Muscle Memory Exercise (MME): G♭ (Concert E)**
1. <u>Without playing</u> your instrument, Practice fingering *B♭* to *C♭*.
2. <u>Without playing</u> your instrument Practice fingering *C♭* to *D♭*.
3. Practice fingering the MME [*B♭-C♭-D♭-C♭-B♭*] 4 times on your instrument.

 **Practice to Performance (PTP)**
1. Play the PTP exercise 4 times.
2. Turn to page 21 and play PTP exercise #6.

19

B♭ Bass Clarinet

# C♭ (Concert A) Major Scale
## (Enharmonic B)

**BEAD Great Chicago Fire**
Go through the order of flats until you get to the name of your key and add one more. That will give you all the flats in the key signature.

Concert Pitch _____

Name of your scale

_____

Name the notes of the Scale:

___ ___ ___ ___ ___ ___ ___ ___

Key Signature: Name the flats

___ ___ ___ ___ ___ ___ ___

1. Write the key signature, measure bars and choose a time signature.
2. Write the scale using music notation. Use different note values to create a scale song.

### Memory Tip

Key of C♭: **Repeat to yourself or out loud:**
C♭ has 7 flats, C♭ has 7 flats – B♭ E♭ A♭ D♭ G♭ C♭ F♭
I "C" (see) all flats.

 **Muscle Memory Exercise (MME): C♭ (Concert A)**
1. Without playing your instrument, Practice fingering E♭ to F♭.
2. Without playing your instrument Practice fingering F♭ to G♭.
3. Practice fingering the MME [E♭-F♭-G♭-F♭-E♭] 4 times on your instrument.

 **Practice to Performance (PTP)**
1. Play the PTP exercise 4 times.
2. Turn to page 21 and play PTP exercise #7.

20

Bb Bass Clarinet

#  PTP Exercises for all Keys

**F (Concert E♭)**
1.

**B♭ (Concert A♭)**
2.

**E♭ (Concert D♭)**
3.

**A♭ (Concert G♭)**
4.

**D♭ (Concert C♭)**
5.

**G♭ (Concert E)**
6.

**C♭ (Concert A)**
7.

Bb Bass Clarinet

 **PTP Exercises for all Keys**

C (Concert B♭)

1.

G (Concert F)

2.

D (Concert C)

3.

A (Concert G)

4.

E (Concert D)

5.

B (Concert A)

6.

F# (Concert E)

7.

C# (Concert B)

8.

# All Major Scales (continued)